C000001080

1 MONTH OF
FREE
READING

at
www.ForgottenBooks.com

By purchasing this book you are eligible for one month membership to ForgottenBooks.com, giving you unlimited access to our entire collection of over 1,000,000 titles via our web site and mobile apps.

To claim your free month visit:
www.forgottenbooks.com/free899978

ISBN 978-0-266-85615-3
PIBN 10899978

This book is a reproduction of an important historical work. Forgotten Books uses state-of-the-art technology to digitally reconstruct the work, preserving the original format whilst repairing imperfections present in the aged copy. In rare cases, an imperfection in the original, such as a blemish or missing page, may be replicated in our edition. We do, however, repair the vast majority of imperfections successfully; any imperfections that remain are intentionally left to preserve the state of such historical works.

Thurber's
Annual
Catalogue of
Seeds and
Plants.

• • •

THURBER'S

Annual Catalogue of

Seeds and Plants

.. 1900 ..

• • •

To the Public:

My annual Catalogue for 1900 is now before you, and in presenting this list to you, I am confident that I have enumerated only the best varieties of Vegetable and Flower seeds.

I thank my many patrons for the favors shown me in the past, and would ask those who have never dealt with me, to compare prices and test the quality of my seeds, with those whom they have formerly dealt and trust that from old and new customers I will receive my share of your patronage.

My aim has been to deal only in the best quality of seeds: it will be my purpose in the future.

There are so many reasons why the best seeds do not always germinate, that it must be distinctly understood that my seeds are not under any guarantee for the productiveness of the crop.

WILLIAM R. THURBER,

Brooklyn, Conn.

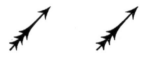

Seeds by Mail, Freight or Express.

Flower or Vegetable Seeds ordered by the packet, ounce or quarter pound will be seut by mail at catalogue prices. When Vegetable Seeds are ordered by mail in quantities of one-half pound and upwards, purchasers must send eight cents per pound for postage. When Peas and Beans are ordered by the quart, by mail, add fifteen cents per quart; Corn, add ten cents per quart.

About Ordering.

In ordering, please write your name, post-office and state plainly. Remittances should be made either by money order on Brooklyn, Conn., registered letter or bank check, payable to my order. Remittances made in any otehr way are at the risk of the sender.

My Greenhouse facilities give me the best opportunity for constant tests of all seeds in my hands.

Market Gardners using large quantities of vegetable seeds and plants, may be greatly benefited by sending me their lists to be priced before buying elsewhere.

Shipment of Plants.

I will send plants by mail, as heretofore; but I would here impress upon my patrons the fact that no plant should be sent by mail to any point where an express office reaches, as larger and finer plants and more of them for the same amount can be sent by express; extra plants are always included that are of more value than the cost of expressage.

I MAKE NO CHARGE FOR BOXES OR PACKING. All orders should be addressed to

WILLIAM R. THURBER, Brooklyn, Conn.

Sowing Flower Seeds.

In sowing all small seeds, care should be taken to have the soil mellow and fine and the seeds should be covered very lightly—in fact the smallest of them should be sown and the soil merely pressed with a board or the hand.

Hardy Annuals may be sown in the open ground from the time the ground is well settled in the spring till late in the summer for succession.

Half-Hardy Annuals should not be sown in open ground till after settled weather and biting frosts are past.

Tender Annuals must not be sown in open ground before all frost is past and the weather is warm and summer-like.

All Annuals may be forwarded early in hotbeds or the window, but the best satisfaction results in open ground.

Biennials and Perennials are best sown in shallow boxes and set out into pots or boxes; and finally, when strong, placed in permanent positions where they are to flower

SPECIAL OFFER

—ON—

FLOWER SEEDS.

As an additional inducement to individuals who desire to possess a large collection, or for the formation of clubs for the same object, we offer to send by mail free of postage, to any address in the United States or Canada, the following:

Purchasers remitting $1 may select to the amount of $ 1.40
      "   "   2   "   "   3.00
      "   3   "   "   5.00
      "   5   "   "   10.00

REMEMBER this discount is on flower seeds only.

In sending orders for Flower Seeds by mail, it will only be necessary to give the date of the Catalogue from which the selection was made, and the NUMBER instead of the names of the varieties.

General List of Flower Seeds.

ANNUALS grow, bloom and die the first year from seed.

BIENNIALS bloom the second year from seed and then die; though many, if sown early in the spring, will flower the first year.

PERENNIALS bloom the second year from seed, and continue to grow and bloom for many years.

ALL FLOWER SEEDS SENT FREE BY MAIL ON RECEIPT OF PRICE.

ABRONIA.

Brilliant trailing plants with Verbena like heads, producing a rich, flowery carpet from July to October. Hardy annuals.

1 **Umbellata.** Rosy pink, packet 5c

ACROCLINUM.

One of the best everlastings, suitable for winter bouquets: half-hardy annuals.

2 **Mixed, Single** 1 foot....pkt. 5c
3 **Mixed, Double** ....pkt. 5c

ADLUMIA: Mountain Fringe.

An attractive climbing plant, with pale-green foliage, bearing small, flesh-colored blossoms; hardy annuals.

4 **Adlumia Cirrhosa** Flesh white 15 feet.......... ....pkt 5c

AGERATUM.

Very valuable for bouquets; lasting long in bloom. Half-hardy annuals. Height. 3—4 foot.

5 **Mixed** Dwarf; blue and white .... pkt. 5c

ALYSSUM.

Modest little plants for edging and border, its flowers being highly prized for bouquets.

6 **Sweet** Pure white, very sweet, hardy annuals, 1 foot. Per ounce, 25 cts........................ Pkt. 5c
7 **Tom Thumb** This is one of the finest plants for edging and low beds, flowering for months; pure white; 1-2 foot.... ....: pkt. 5c

AMARANTHUS.

A class of plants valued for their highly ornamented foliage; native of East Indies, requiring a poor, light soil to bring them to perfection, half-hardy annuals.

8 **Tricolor** (Joseph's Coat.) Red, yellow and green foliage.....pkt. 5c

9 **Salicifolius** (Fountain Plant) Drooping, willow-shaped leaves, tipped with orange, carmine and bronze, ...pkt 5c

ANTIRRHINUM Snapdragon.

The Snapdragon or Antirrhinum, is one of the most useful and showy border plants; half hardy perennials,

10 **Tall Varieties mixed** 2 ft.

.............................pkt 5c

ACQUILEGIA.

The universally admired "Columbine," of almost every conceivable color and variation; hardy perennials. .

11 **Varieties Mixed**........pkt. 5c

GERMAN ASTER.

This beautiful class of plants now constitutes one of our finest autumnal flowers. Plant the seed early, in hotbeds, or in pots or boxes, and transplant to a deep rich soil six to twelve inches apart.

12 **Bettridge's Quilled** An improved form of Quilled Aster. The flowers are of fine form and brilliant colors; 2 ft.............. ... pkt. 5c

13 **Comet** Mixed colors. Those beautiful Asters have long twisted petals formed into a loose, yet dense half globe; flowers large....pkt. 10c

14 **Peony Flowered Perfection** Flowers large and double; choice mixed colors. 2 ft..........pkt. 10c

15 **Victoria** Flowers very large, perfectly double, forming a compact bush; 2 feet high; choice mixed colors.................... ... pkt. 10c

16 **Semples** Snow white; a most beautiful variety; flowers are very large .... pkt. 10c

PEONY ASTER. No. 14,

17 **Dwarf Pyramidal Bouquet.** Height from 12 to 15 inches; a very free blooming variety; mixed colors .... pkt. 10c

18 **Semple's Branching** Super-

'ior to any other class of late flowering Branching Aster; mixed colors 2 ft high..................pkt. 10c

19 **Dwarf Chrysanthemum Flowered** This is a valuable late variety, coming in after many other varieties are gone. Mixed. 9 inches high.................. ... pkt. 10c

20 **Mignon Asters** The plants are semi-dwarf and bear very double flowers with deeply imbricated petals mixed colors.... ....pkt. 10c

21 **Ball-Shaped or "Jewel" Asters.** The flowers are perfecly round or ball shaped, densely double, short incurved petals. 2 ft. Mixed colors......................pkt. 10c

Coll. of Asters as imported

22 **Comet** in six separate colors 40c

23 **Jewel** in six separate colors 40c

24 **Truffaut's Poeny Flowered Perfection** Twelve separate colors...................... ......60c

25 **Victoria** In twelve separate colors...........................60c

BALSAMS.

An old and popular favorite of which our present stock is a great improvement on old sorts, being usually double and finely colored and variegated halt-hardy annuals.

26 **Double Camelia Flowered** Finest mixed colors, 2 ft.....pkt 5c

27 **Double White Perfection** Very fine, 2 ft.. ....pkt. 10c

28 **Rose Flowered.** Very double, Mixed color............... . pkt. 5c

29 **Mixed Balsams.......**pkt. 5c

COLLECTION OF BALSAMS.

30 **Double Camelia Flowered.** In twelve separate colors........50c

31 **Rose Flowered.** In twelve different colors............... ......50c

BELLIS. Double Daisy.

A well known perennial. They are admirable plants for making edgings, etc. Half-hardy perennial.

32 **Perennis.** Extra fine; saved from named flowers; 1-4 foot, pkt. 10c

33 **Snowball.** Double; White.10c

34 **Longfellow.** Double; pink .10c

BROWALLIA.

The Browallia is very prettv for bouquets. Half-hardy annuals.

35 **Elata Major.** Blue and white Mixed ....pkt. 5c

CACALIA Tassel Flowers.

A beautiful annual, with a profusion of scarlet and orange tassel-shaped flowers, blooming from July to October

36 **Mixed.** Yellow and scarlet...5c

CALENDULA

A very showy free-flowering genus of plants, producing a pretty effect in beds or borders. Hardy annuals. pkt.

37 **Le Proust.** Nankeen colored,

38 **Meteor.** Yellow with light orange striped flowers..............5c

39 **Pongei.** Double; white.....5c

CALLIOPSIS.

A very showy border plant, producing flowers in shades of yellow, orange, crimson and brown. Tall varieties. Hardy annual; height 2 feet.

40 **Mixed.** pkt.5c

CANDYTUFT, Iberis.

Old, popular and beautiful. Hardy annuals. pkt.

41 **White.** Sweet scented.... ...5c

42 **Purple**......................5c

43 **Empress.** A most beautiful candytuft; pure white 5c

44 **DARK CRIMSON**..........5c

45 **Fine Mixed**..... ....5c

CANNA. Indian shot.

Extremely ornamental and stately foliage plants, producing a decidedly tropical appearance. Flowers bright and attractive. Half-hardy perennials.

46 **French Mixed, Large Flowing.** pkt.10c

CANTERBURY BELLS.

Campanula Medium

Well known and deservedly popular Hardy perennials. pkt.

47 **Single Mixed** 5c

48 **Double Mixed**...... ... ... 5c

CARNATION.

A class of popular favorites, most of them deliciously fragrant, and with colors extremely rich and beautiful. Half-hardy perennials.

49 **Marguerite**. These are the most abundant bloomers of the carnation pinks; the flowers are of many shades
• of red, pink, white, variagated. pkt.......... .... 10c

50 **Mixed**. For border culture; double pkt.10c

CELOSIA.

These are exeedingly brilliant and attractive half-hardy annuals never fail to please if grown from first quality seed. pkt.

51 **Pyramidalis Mixed.** Three

feet high................... ..... 5c

52 **Cristata.** Nana Mixed ....;..5c

53 **Plumosa Mixed.** 5c

CENTAUREA.

Valuable silver foliage plants, very effective for basket. vases and window boxes, as well as the finest silver-leaved plants for contrasting with Coleus and other dark-leaved plants, in massed beds; half-hardy perennials.

54 **Gymnocarpa.** Silver foliage; 1 1-2 feet...................pkt: 10c

CHRYSANTHEMUMS.

A well known garden favorite. The annual varieties are among the most showy and effective of summer flowering plants.

55 **Mixed.** Annual varieties. pkt. 5c

56 **Indicum.** Large flowering; mixed; half-hardy perennials pkt. 15c

57 **Japonicum.** Fringed varieties; mixed colors; ha.f-hardy perennials .... pkt.. 15c

COBEA

A most beautiful climber, of rapid growth; producing many large, bell-shaped flowers. Plant the seed in moist earth, edgewise Half-hardy perennials.

58 **Scandens.** Rich violet blue; 25 feet.....................pkt. 10c

CONVOLVULUS.

The most popular annual in cultivation, for in this is included the well-known Morning Glóry. The minor varieties are well suited for bedding; they attain an average of height of one foot. Half-hardy annuals. pkt.

59 **Minor Tricolor.** Mixed 5c

60 **Major.** (Morning Glory.) Mixed; per ounce 15c .... pkt. 5c

No. 60 CONVOLVULUS.

COSMOS.

The plants grow 4 to 6 feet high, and

Left margin (faded fragments):
...5e
...5e
...5e

i. very
vindow
-leaved
us and
massed

foliage;
pkt. 10c
Is.

e. The
he most
r flower-

s. pkt. 5c
ing;
pkt. 15c
varieties;
perennials
pkt. 15c

of rapid
re, bell-
ia moist
rennials.
blue;
pkt. 10c

i cultiva-
the well-
minor va-
ing; they
ne foot.
pkt.
d 5c
Mixed;
pkt. 5c

a. and

COSMOS.

are literally covered in the autumn with large single dahlia-like flowers, ranging through shades of rose, purple, white, etc ; splendid for cutting purposes ; feathery foliage.

61 **Large Flowering**. Mixed colors. . . ..pkt. 5c

62 **Early Flowering**. White. pkt. ....:.....10c

CYCLAMEN.

Beautiful winter and spring-flowering plants, with sweet scented, singular shaped flowers ; for culture in pots. Half-hardy perennials.

63 **Cyclamen Persicum**. Finest varieties; mixed.................10c

CYPRESS VINE Impomæ Quamoclit.

A tender, climbing annual, with graceful foliage ; seed should not be planted in the ground before the last of May or the first of June.

64 **Mixed**. 5c

DAHLIA

Seeds saved from the very finest named sorts in cultivation. Seed sown in early spring will produce plants that bloom from August until frost. Half-hardy perennials. pkt.

65 **Double Mixed**.............10c

66 **Single Mixed**...............5c

DATURA. Trumpet flower,

Hardy annuals, with double purple and white flowers; height 2 feet. pkt.

67 **Datura Fastuosa**.........5c

DIGITALIS. Fox Glove.

A very hardy biennial, with flower stems at least 3 feet in heighth, bearing flowers of an iregular bell-shape ; color white and different shades of purple and red.

68 **Fox Glove**. Finest colors and shades mixed...... ....pkt. 5c

DIANTHUS.

A beautiful genus of easy culture, embracing some of the most popular flowers in cultivation. Their free blooming quality, together with the exquisite blending of colors and richness of single flowers, places them at the head of all bedding plants that are quickly grown from seed. Hardy annuals.

69 **Chinensis**. Fine mixed double flowers.....................pkt. 5c

70 **Imperialis.** Double Imperial pink, extra fine mixed ...... pkt. 5c

71 **Heddewigii Flore Pleno.** Double Japan pink, very showy 1 ft. high............ ....pkt. 5c

72 **Diadematus.** Dwarf of compact habit. Flowers very large of various colors; double.......pkt. 5c

73 **The Bride** Single large flowers; white with violet center......pkt. 5c

74 **Eastern Queen.** Beautifully marbled; single..............pkt. 5c

75 **Crimson Belle.** Rich crimson color; flowers of very large size and substance; single ....pkt. 5c

76 **All Kinds.** Mixed.. .... pkt. 5c

ESCHSCHOLTZIA.

California Poppy.

Extremely free-flowering and showy hardy annuals, of rich and beautiful colors.   pkt.

77 **Finest Varieties.** Mixed 5c

78 **DOUBLE MIXED**.........5c

Eternal or Everlasting Flowers. [See Helichrysum and Acroclinium.]

GERANIUM. Pelagonium.

These well known garden favorites are as indispensable for indoor as for outdoor decorations, and should be extensively cultivated. Perennials.   pkt.

79 **Zonale.** Finest mixed... ...10c

GILIA.

Free-flowering hardy annual, producing clusters of small, bright, delicate flowers; pretty in small clumps; flowers continually.

80 **All Varieties.** Mixed... pkt. 5c

GLOXINIA.

A superb genus of stove plants producing in great profusion flowers of the richest and most beautiful hue; thrives best in sandy peat and loom; hot-house bulbs.   pkt.

81 **Choice.** Mixed .....:......20c

GODETIA.

All the varieties of the Godetia are well worth growing, the profuseness of bloom and delicate tints of color have rendered them universal favorites. pkt.

82 **Fine Mixed.** All colors. ... 5c

GOURD. Mock Orange.

Rapid growing plants, useful for covering unsightly spots, producing beautiful and often very curious many-shaped fruits.

83 **Gourds.** A splendid assortment of best varieties ....pkt. 5c

GYPSOPHILA.

Elegant little plant, adapted for rock work; baskets or edgings.

84 **Murallis.** A charming little plant, covered with pretty little pink flowers; hardy annuals......pkt. 5c

HELIANTHUS. Sunflower.

Very handsome varieties of Sunflower remarkable for their stately growth and the brilliancy and size of their flowers.

85 **Californicus.** Extra large and double; 5 feet high ....pkt. 5c

HELICHRYSUM. Eternal Flower.

An effective and indispensible everlasting flower, both for garden, ornamental and winter bouquets; hardy annuals.   pkt.

86 **Finest Colors.** Mixed...... 5c

HOLLYHOCK.

Our seed of this old favorite has been saved from an unsurpassed collection of the most rich and brilliant colors; hardy perennials.

87 **Hollyhock.** Extra choice; double, of great beauty; splendid English varieties mixed ....pkt. 10c

LATHYRUS. See Sweet Peas.

LARKSPUR. Delphinum.

Beautiful and well-known plants of the easiest culture, and productive of showy flowers of a great variety of colors; pleasing and useful for cutting; hardy annuals.

88 **Dwarf Rocket.** Finest mixed; double .... pkt. 5c

89 **Tall Rocket.** Finest mixed double.... ....pkt. 5c

90 **Emperor.** Varieties mixed pkt. 5c

91 **Mixed.**...... .... 5c

LINUM.

Neat and beautiful half-hardy annual with bright and handsome flowers all summer, produced in abundance.

92 **Graniflorum Rubrum** pkt. Bright crimson; 18 inches........5c

LOBELIA

A class of plants of great beauty and usefulness; equally well adapted for pots, baskets, vases, or for border culture; half-hardy annuals.

93 **Crystal Palace Compacta.** A beautiful blue variety......pkt. 5c

94 **Speciosa.** The most effective of Lobelias.......... ....pkt. 5c

95 **Erinus.** Mixed.........pkt. 5c

MAURANDIA.

A beautiful, rather (delicate and graceful climber, with flowers blue, white and mauve, of various shades.

96 **Finest Mixed.....** ....pkt. 10c

MARIGOLD. Tagetes.

The French and African Marigolds are among the most elegant and beautiful of our annuals; half-hardy annuals.

97 **African Quilled.** Finest double; 2 feet high..................5c

98 **French Dwarf.** Mixed; double; 1 foot high................ 5c

99 **French Striped.** Striped gold 5c

MARVEL OF PERU. Mirabilis.

The well-known "Evening Beauty" "Four O'clock," "Belle of the night," etc.. of varied colors and striped; very fragrant and free flowering.

100 **Jalapa.** Finest mixed, including beautiful striped sorts....pkt. 5c

MIGNONETTE.

A well-known favorite, highly esteemed for its fragrance; if well thinned out as soon as the plants are large enough they will grow stronger and produce larger spikes of bloom; hardy annuals.

101 **Mignonette.** (Reseda Odorata) per ounce 15c....:..........pkt. 5c

102 **Machet.** A dwarf French variety with broad spikes of very fragrant red flowers; one of the best varieties. 10c

103 **Hybrid Spiral.** This variety of Mignonette is a strong grower and fragrant 5c

104 **Golden Queen.** Literally a mass of fragrant gold.... ....5c

MIMOSA.

105 Pudica. A curious and interesting plant. the leaves closing if touched or shaken, but soon opening again; half-hardy annuals.......... ....5c

MORNING GLORY.

(See Convolvulus)

106 **Japan Morning Glory.** One of our most beautiful climbers. The flowers are of gigantic size; they attain a height of from 30 to 50 ft. mixed colors..... ....pkt. 10c

MIMULUS. Monkey Flower.

Very striking and beautiful, tender looking plants, excellent for pots, boxes, baskets or open ground culture.

107 **Moschatus.** (Musk Plant.) Yellow; one-half foot high....pkt. 5c

108 **Choice Mixed**. Finest spotted sorts.................. .. ..pkt. 5c

MYRSIPHYLLUM. Smilax.

Of late this has become very popular, being, as it is, one of the most graceful and beautiful climbers in cultivation; for all occasions it is the best adapted of all plants for dressing the hair. pkt.

109 **Asparagoides**. White; 7 ft 10c

MYOSOTIS. Forget-me-not.

The different species of this popular genus are all very beautiful, and too well known to need recommendation; they succeed best in moist situations.|

110 **Disitisflora**. Large, sky-blue flowers; very early and free blooming ....pkt. 5c

111 **Semperflorens** · Flowering from early spring till autumn, White; 6 inches....................pkt. 10c

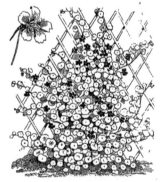

NASTURTIUMS.

For covering lattice-work and trellises, old clumps, etc., the tall Nasturtiums are adapted. The dwarf Nasturtiums are excellent for bedding, forming beautifully-rounded clumps, covered with showy flowers. pkt.

112 **Luteum**. Rich yellow, no blotches. oz. 15c. ....pkt. 5c

113 **Schillingi**. Yellow maroon blotches. oz. 15c ....pkt. 5c

114 **Tall Rose**. Oz. 15c......pkt. 5c

115 " **White**. Pearl. Oz. 15c..5c

116 " **Scarlet**. Oz. 15c......5c

117 " **Orange**. Oz. 15c......5c

118 " **Crimson**. Oz. 15c.. ..5c

119 **Maroon**. Oz. 15c.... .... .5c

120 **Scarlet and Gold**. Yellow foliage; flowers crimson-scarlet....10c

121 **Tall Mixed**. 10 feet, 1-4 lb. 30c Oz. 10c ....pkt. 5c

122 **Empress of India**. · Dark foliage; flowers crimson dwarf....5c

123 **Tom Thumb**, Orange, Oz. 15c 5c

124 **Tom Thumb**. Scarlet. Oz. 15c 5c

125 **Tom Thumb**. White. Oz. 15c....................... .5c

126 **Tom Thumb**. Maroon. Oz. 15c 5c

127 **Luteum**. Light yellow, no blotches. Oz. 15c 5c

128 **Golden King**. Golden, Maroon blotches. Oz. 20c 5c

129 **Tom Thumb**. Mixed. 1 foot Oz. 15c 1-4 lb. 40c..............5c

PANSY. Viola Tricolor.

The pansy is a general favorite. The flowers are in the greatest perfection in May or June. Seed sown in August in the open border will come up readily in a few weeks. They require to be covered during the winter with ever-green boughs or a cold frame. If sown early in spring they will bloom the first season. Hardy perennials:

130 **English**. Extra select; large flowers. pkt.
..................................15c

131 **Giant Trimardeau**. Mixed colors.................. 10c

132 **Odier, and Cassiers**. Very large flowers and distinctively blotched, mixed colors........ ..... 15c

133 **Emperor William**. New, brilliant ultramarine blue, violet eye ....~........5c

134 **King of the Blacks**. Almost coal black ; true to seed... 5c

135 **White**. Snowflake ; choice for cemetery use......................5c

136 **Yellow**. Constant and fine.. 5c

137 **Mixed** Fine quality........10c

138 **Good Mixed**........... ....5c

PETUNIA

Profuse blooming, extremely showy and indispensable garden favorites ; half-hardy annuals.

139 **Petunia Hybrida**. Large flowering, single, fringed, mixed pkt. 20c

140 **Petunia Hybrida**. Double fringed ; mixed ....:.....pкt. 25c

141 **Hybrida Flore Pleno**. Finest mixed ; will produce a large percentage of double flowers....... pkt. 20c

142 **Fine Mixed**. Single...pkt. 5c

PHLOX DRUMMONDI.

This magnificent genus of plants is unrivalled for richness and brilliancy of color ; profusion and duration of blooming ; they are unsurpassed for bedding mixed border, succeed in light, rich soil ; hardy annuals.

143 **Star Shaped Phlox**. Regular star-like form 10c

144 **Double Mixed** 10c

145 **Alba Flore**. Pure white....10c

146 **Grandiflora Splendens**. Large flowers, mixed............10c

147 **Coccinea**. Deep scarlet....10c

148 **Mixed**. First quality..... .. 5c

149 **Decussata**. Perennial, mixed 10c

POPPY.

A tribe of remarkably showy, free-flowering plants, growing freely in any soil ; hardy annuals.

150 **Peony Flowered**. Mixed double ; 2 feet................pkt. 5c

151 **Umbrosum**. Color a rich vermillion, with black spots on each petal................................5c

152 **Danebrog**. New and large, bright scarlet 5c

153 **Tulip Poppy**. A magnificent new species, resembling scarlet tulips 5c

154 **Single Mixed**............. 5c

155 **Iceland Single Mixed**. The delicate, fragrant flowers are exceedingly beautiful, and with their long stems are well suited for cutting. The plants are perfectly hardy, easily cultivated, and the lovely white, yellow and orange-red flowers are in bloom from early summer until fall. Hardy perennial, blooming the first year from seed................. pkt. 10c

PORTULACCA.

In praise of these charming flowers it is impossible to speak too highly. The double Portulacca is one of the most showy and desirable of annuals.

Hardy annuals.

156 **Grandiflora**. Finest mixed; double..................... pkt. 10c

157 **Splendid.** Single, mixed, all colors....................... pkt. 5c

PRIMULA, Chinese Primrose.

Charming, pro-fuse - flowering plants indispensable for winter and spring decorations in the conservatory; succeed best in sandy loam and leaf mould; tender perennials.

158 **Sinensis Fimbriata.** Single fringed; mixed colors pkt. 25c

159 **Sinensis Fimbriata.** Single fringed; pure white pkt. ... .25c

160 **Sinensis Fimbriata.** Single fringed; red .... pkt. 25c

RICINUS. Castor Oil Bean.

Stately, ornamental plants of elegant foliage; splendid as single plant on large lawns; hardy annuals.

161 **Ricinus.** Mixed varieties pkt. 5c

SALPIGLOSSIS.

Very ornamental and useful plants for late summer and autumn decorations, producing curiously penciled and mar-ble funnel shaped flowers of easy culture; half-hardy annuals.

162 **Large Flowered.** Finest mixed; extra............... pkt. 5c

SALVIA. Sage.

Magnificent bedding plants producing large spike of bloom from July until frost, also well adapted for winter blooming; half-hardy perennials.

163 **Splendens.** Brilliant Scarlet .. .. pkt. 5c

SWEET PEAS.

Lathyrus.

The Sweet Peas are among the most popular annuals which enrich the garden; they may be planted and trained on sticks the same as the common peas, or they may be sown along the sides of the fences forming an ornamental covering. In any situation t h e y are always admired.

166 **Boreatton Maroon.** Oz. 10c. pkt. 5c

167 **Blanche Ferry** pink and white..Oz. 10c ....pkt. 5c

168 **Emily Henderson.** White ..Oz 10c .... pkt. 5c

169 **Striped.** Red and white. Oz. 10c. pkt. 5c

170 **Invincible Scarlet.** Bright scarlet and fragrant. Oz. 10c .... pkt. 5c

171 **Vesuvius.** Spotted maroon. Oz 10c ....pckt. 5c

SCABIOSA, or Mourning Bride.

Sweet Scabiosa.

Handsome, showy plants for mixed borders. Flowers beautifully variagated hardy annnals.

164 **Atropurea. Major.** Finest double; mixed..............pkt. 5c

165 **Dwarf.** Double mixed..pkt. 5c

172 **Butterfly.** White laced with Blue; fragrant. .. Oz. 10c..pkt. 5c

173 **Princess Beatrice,** Rose color .... Oz. 10c .... . .pkt. 5c

174 **Fairy Queen.** White and pink. ....Oz. 10c........... pkt 5c

175 **Crown Princess.** Blush. Oz. 10c .... pkt. 5c

176 **Lemon Queen.** White, lemon

tinted. Oz. 10c ....pkt. 5c
177 **Katherine Tracy.** Soft pink,
Oz. 10c...... ....pkt. 5c
178 **Splendour.** Rose and crimson
Oz. 10c ....pkt. 5c
179 **Lottie Eckford.** White edged
blue Oz. 10c. ....pkt. 5c
180 **Firefly.** Crimson scarlet. Oz.
10c .. ..pkt. 5c
181 **Mixed.** Per lb. 50c , 1-4 lb. 20c
............Oz. 10c .... pkt. 5c
182 **Eckford's Mixed.** Large flowers. per lb. 60c., 1-4 lb. 20c., oz. 10c
.... pkt. 5c
183 **Everlasting or Perennials.**
Finest mixed ....pkt. 5c
184 **15 Distinct Varieties.**....50c
185 **Cupid.** Dwarf white....pkt. 5c
186 **Cupid.** Dwarf pink.....pkt. 5c
STOCKS. Ten Weeks.
Mathiola.
Especially valuable on acccount of
their long flowering period, and bright
constant flowers produced in abundance.
187 **Finest Mixed.** Dwarf German.
.... pkt. 5c
188 **Large Flowering.** Finest
mixed.... ....pkt. 10c
189 **Pure White** ....pkt. 10c
190 **Dwarf Pyramidal.** Best
stock in cultivation. Mixed pkt. 10c
191 **Wallflower Leaved.** Finest
dwarf mixed ....pkt. 10c
SWEET WILLIAM.
Dianthus Barbatus.
A very beautiful and well-known
class of plants, of extreme richness and
diversity of color. The varieties have
been greatly improved of late years.
Hardy Perennials.
192 **Fine Mixed.**...........pkt. 5c

193 **Double Flowering.** Finest
mixed, from a splendid collection of
double flowers ... .pkt 5c

THUNBERGIA.

A pretty genus of climbers of slender
and rapid growth, with gay and justly
admired flowers, freely produced either
as a house or border plant; tender annuals.
194 **Finest Mixed.** Buff, white, orange, etc............... .....pkt. 5c

VERBENA.

A charming genus of universally admired and easily cultivated plants, sim-
ply requiring the treatment of half-
hardy annuals to have them bloom
during the summer. Tender perennials.
195 **Hybrida.** From the finest
named sorts, Extra mixed....pkt. 15c
196 **Fine Mixed**..........pkt. 10c
197 **Good Mixed**..........pkt. 5c

WHITLAVIA.

Very pretty, free-flowering hardy annuals; producing exquisite bell-shaped
flowers, easily cultivated.
198 **Mixed.** Blue and white ..pkt. 5c

ZINNIA.

Extremely showy late summer and
autumn flowering plants of great richness and variety of color, rivaling in
size and doubleness moderate-sized
Dahlias.
199 **Eligans Flore Pleno.** Extra choice double, Mixed......pkt. 5c
200 **8 Varieties Zinnia**...... 30c
201 **Zinnia Elegans Grandiflora Mixed**............... pkt. 10c

SELECT LIST

—— OF ——

Vegetable Seeds.

EMBRACING

All of the Leading Varieties

Suited to the wants of the Market Gardener, as well as the Family Gardens.

Of course we cannot warrant them to produce a perfect crop, as we do not have control of their planting nor the cultivation of the crop, and often the weather is so unfavorable as to either destroy the best seeds or to badly injure a growing crop.

When Vegetable seeds are ordered by freight or express in quantities of one-half pound and upwards, they will be sent at catalogue prices, but when ordered by mail in the same quantities, add at the rate of eight cents per pound for postage.

When beans or peas are ordered by mail by the quart or pint, add at the rate of fifteen cents per quart: Corn, add at the rate of ten cents per quart.

ASPARAGUS.

Collossal. The standard variety, pkt. 5c., oz. 10c., 1-4 lb. 20c.

BEANS. Dwarf or Bush 10c. per packet postpaid by mail. Add 15c. per quart if sent by mail.

Improved Early Red Valentine Early, productive, tender and of best quality. Pt. 15c., qt. 25c., pk. $1.75.

Dwarf Horticultural. A bush variety of the well-known Horticultural Pole bean. Pt. 15c., qt. 25c., pk $1.75

White Seeded Wax. Variety with wax-like pods. The seeds are pure white. It is very productive and an excellent variety. Pt. 15c., qt. 30c., pk. $2.00.

Improved Rustless Golden Wax The pods are produced in profusion, are quite stringless, very white wax-like. Pt. 15c., qt. 30c., pk. $1.75.

Wardwell's Dwarf Kidney Wax This variety is very hardy. It produces a heavy crop of purely wax pods, not liable to rust or blister. The pods are thick and tender. Pt. 15c., qt. 30c., pk. $2.00.

Golden Wax. It is an entirely distinct variety, a week or ten days earlier than the black wax. The pods are large, brittle and stringless. Pt.

25 Pkts. Vegetable Seeds for $1.00.

15c., qt. 25c., pk. $1.75.

Henderson's Bush Lima. It grows in a compact bush form about 18 inches high, and produces enormous crops of delicious beans. Qt 30c., pt. 15c.

Burpee's Bush Lima. This is a bush form of the well-known large White Lima Bean. It is very fixed in its bush character, growing to a uniform height of about 20 inches. The pods obtain as many beans as the Pole Limas. Pt. 20c., qt. 35c.

BEANS. Pole or Running.

10c per pkt. postpaid by mail. Add 15c per qt. if to go by mail.

Large Lima. Considered the best of all beans. Universally grown for shell beans, dry or green. Qt. 30c, pt. 20c.

Early Dutch Case Knife. Early and productive. Qt. 30c., pt. 15c.

Jersey Extra Early Lima. Every one desiring a Pole Lima Bean should plant the Jersey Extra Early, as it combines better than any other, quantity, quality and earliness. Pt. 20c., qt. 35c.

Horticultural or Speckled Cranberry. Excellent for use, green or dry. Qt. 25c., pt 15c.

BEETS.

The soil should be rich, deep and mellow; plant the seeds in rows 12 or 15 inches apart.

If by mail in quantities of 1-2 lb. and upwards, add at the rate of 8c per lb.

Edmunds Early Turnip Beet. Grows small tops, the beets are smooth, round and of good size, the flesh very dark red and remarkably sweet and tender; one of the finest

table beets grown. Pkt. 5c., oz. 10c., 1-4 lb. 15c, lb. 42c.

Long Smooth Blood Red. An excellent late variety; a great improvement on the common Long blood. Pkt. 5c., oz 10c, 1-4 lb. 15c., lb. 42c.

Egyptian Turnip Beet. Earliest in cultivation. Pkt 5c, oz 10c., 1-4 lb. 15c., lb. 42c.

Eclipse Beet. Nearly as early as the Egyptian, of much finer quality; round dark crimson. Pkt. 5c., oz. 10c., 1-4 lb. 15c, lb. 42c

EARLY BLOOD TURNIP.

The standard early sort; a late keeper. Pkt. 5c., oz. 10c, 1-4 lb. 15c., lb. 42c.

Lentz. It is as early as the Egyptian of fine dark red color, a very small top, tender and sweet, very productive. Pkt. 5c, oz. 10c., 1-4 lb. 15c., lb. 42c

Bastian's Extra Early Turnip. An early variety, of handsome shape, deep red color and superior quality. Pkt. 5c., oz. 10c, 1-4 lb. 15c., lb. 42c

Dewing's Blood Turnip. Deep Blood-red, fine form and flavor; very early, good market sort. Pkt. 5c., oz. 10c., 1-4 lb. 15c., lb. 42c

25 Pkts. Vegetable Seeds for $1.00.

Varieties Adapted to Growing For Feeding Stock.

Sow in April and May. 6 to 8 pounds to an acre.

White Sugar. Very large size and excellent for feeding. Oz. 8c., 1-4 lb. 10c., lb. 30c.

Champion Yellow Globe.

Smooth, globe-shaped roots, of large size and excellent quality. Oz 8c., 1-4 lb. 10c., lb. 30c.

Norbiton Giant Long Red Mangel.

A great improvement on the common long red, producing immense crops on good soil. Oz 8c., 1-4 lb. 10c., lb. 30.

CABBAGE.

The cabbage requires a deep, rich soil and thorough working. For early use the plants should be started in a hot-bed or cold frame; but seed for winter cabbage should be sown in a seed-bed early in the spring. Some of the large, late varieties seem to do best if the seed is sown in hills where they are to remain, and in that case sow two or three seeds where each plant is desired, and then pull up all but the strongest. Plant the large varieties 3 feet apart; the small, early sorts from a foot to 18 inches. If by mail in quantities of 1-2 lb, and upwards, add at the rate of 8c. per pound for postage.

Henderson's Early Summer.

It is the earliest of large cabbages. Ten days later than the Wakefield and rarely if ever cracking open when ripe Pkt. 5c., oz. 20c., 1-4 lb. 60c., lb. $2.00.

Henderson Succession. About one week later than the early summer, but it is double the size; good either early or late. Pkt. 5c., oz. 20c. 1-4 lb. 60c., lb. $2.25.

Early Jersey Wakefield. Leading early market variety. The best and most profitable sort. Pkt. 5c., oz. 25c , 1-4 lb. 75c., lb.$3.00.

Early Winningstadt. An excellent variety of good size; sure to head even in poor soil. Pkt. 5c , oz. 15c., 1-4 lb. 35c., lb. $1.25.

Large Late Drum Head. Very large size; sound, compact heads. Pkt. 5c., oz. 15c., 1-4 lb. 40c, lb.$1.50.

Fottler's Improved Brunswick. An excellent second early and late variety. Pkt. 5c., oz. 15c., 1-4 lb. 40c. lb. $1.50.

Stone Mason. Large, compact and of fine quality; late; good keeper. Pkt. 5c., oz. 15c., 1-4 lb. 50c., lb. $1.60.

PREMIUM FLAT DUTCH.
A superior variety; large, of excellent

25 Pkts, Vegetable Seeds for $1.00.

flavor. Pkt. 5c, oz. 15c., 1-4 lb. 40c., lb. $1.50.

Autumn King. The finest late cabbage. Pkt. 5c., oz. 20c., 1-4 lb. 60c., lb. $2.25.

Mammoth Rock Red. Excellent for pickling. Pkt. 5c., oz. 20c., 1-4 lb 60c., lb. $2.25.

CARROTS.

If by mail in quantities of 1-2 pound and upwards, add at the rate of 8c. per pound for postage.

Danvers. A valuable sort; rich shade of orange, smooth. Pkt. 5c. oz. 10c., 1-4 lb. 20c., lb. 55c.

Long Orange. Large size; good for garden or field culture. Pkt. 5c., oz. 10c., 1-4 lb. 20c., lb. 50c.

CAULIFLOWER,

Any soil that will grow early cabbages will grow cauliflower, as their requirements are almost similar.

Henderson's Early Snowball. This variety of Cauliflower has given the greatest satisfaction in all sections; the earliest of the Cauliflowers. It is about one week earlier than any other sort. Every plant forms a head, Pkt. 15c., oz. $2.00.

CELERY.

Sow seeds in a hotbed or in a cold-frame. As soon as the plants are about three inches high, transplant to a nicely prepared bed in the border, setting them four or five inches apart. When some eight inches high and fine, stocky plants, set them in trenches. Earth up a little during the summer, keeping the leaf stocks closely together, so that the soil cannot get between them. Finish earthing up in autumn, and never hoe or earth up in moist weather, nor when plants are moistened with dew. To preserve celery for winter dig trenches a foot in width and as deep as the tops of the plants. Stand the celery in these erect, as it grew, with what dirt adheres to the root, packing closely, but not crowding.

White Plume. In growth it is similar to the half dwarf, but the one quality that recommends it especially above other sorts is that it can be blanched without high banking. Pkt. 5c., oz. 20c.

Pink Plume. New. A variety similar in general character to white plume, but stalks are tinged with pink, making it a wonderfully attractive and beautiful sort. It is equal in quality to the white plume and earlier. Pkt. 5c., oz. 25c.

Henderson's Half Dwarf. One of the best large varieties in culivation. Pkt. 5c., oz. 15c.

CORN.

10c. per pkt. by mail postpaid. Add 10 cents per qt. if sent by mail for postage.

Hickox Hybrid. Popular wherever it is known. It is one or two weeks earlier than Stowell's Evergreen, makes a large attractive ear of very white and handsome grain. The best sort to dry. Pt. 12c., qt. 20c., pk. $1.00.

Cory Early Sweet. It is the earliest of the large red cob varieties that have yet been introduced. Pt. 12c., qt. 20c., pk. $1.00.

White Cob Cory. An extra early variety, identical with Cory Early, except in color. Pt 12c., qt. 20c., pk. $1.00.

Moore's Early Concord. A deli-

25 Pkts. Vegetable Seeds for $1.00.

cate variety; productive. Pt. 12c., qt. 20c., pk. $1.00.

Stowell's Evergreen. The favorite. Very tender and excellent for the table. Pt. 12c., qt. 20c., pk. $1.00.

Potter's Excelsior. The sweetest medium early sweet corn, twelve rowed, white prolific. Excellent for canning.! Pt. 12c., qt. 20c., pk. $1.00.

Perry's Hybrid. Stalks of medium height, bearing two large, twelve or fourteen rowed ears, often have a red cob; cooking very white and tender. Matures a little later than Minnesota. Pt. 12c., qt. 20c., pk. $1.00.

Crosby's Early. Early and a great favorite. Rather small ears but productive and of excellent quality. Pt. 12c., qt. 20c., pk. $1.00.

CUCUMBER.

In this latitude, it is useless to plant in the open ground until nearly the first of June. Make rich hills of well-rotted manure, two feet in diameter, and plant a dozen or more seeds, covering half an inch deep. When all danger from insects is over, pull all but three or four of the strongest plants. The middle of June is early enough to plant for pickling. Make the hills about 6 feet apart·

If by mail in quantities of 1-2 lb. and upwards, add at the rate of 8c. per lb. for postage.

Improved Early White Spine.
A favorite market variety; productive. Pkt. 5c., oz. 10c., 1-4 lb. 15c., lb. 40c.

Early Cluster. An esteemed early variety; grows in clusters; productive. Pkt. 5c., oz. 10c., 1-4 lb. 15c., lb. 40c.

Green Prolific. As a pickling variety is unsurpassed. Pkt. 5c., oz. 10c., 1-4 lb. 15c., lb. 40c.

Nichols' Medium Green. It is exceedingly productive, of medium size, always straight and smooth, The color is dark green, the flesh tender and crisp. Pkt. 5c., oz. 10c., 1-4 lb. 15c., lb. 40c.

Long Green. Produces long fruit of superior quality; firm and crisp. Pkt. 5c., oz. 10c., 1-4 lb. 15c., lb. 40c.

Early Russian. Very early; fruit grows in pairs; hardy and productive. Pkt. 5c., oz. 10c., 1-4 lb. 15c., lb. 45c.

Early Frame. An old, popular variety, Excellent for pickles when small Pkt. 5c., oz. 10c., 1-4 lb. 15c., lb. 40c.

Cool and Crisp. The flesh is peculiarly crisp and tender, and it is one of the very best for table use. Pkt. 5c. oz. 10c., 1-4 lb. 20c., lb. 50c.

EGG PLANT.

The egg plant is tender and requires to be started very early under glass.

25 Pkts. Vegetable Seeds for $1.00.

New York Improved. The leading variety. Pkt. 5c.

LETTUCE.

Lettuce needs a moist, rich soil; rapid growth makes better quality.

Early Curled Simpson. Leading market variety; Pkt. 5c , oz 10c , 1-4 lb. 30c., lb. $1.

Salamander. The best variety for summer use, forming good sized heads; color, light green on outside, white on inside; stands the drought well; very slow to run to seed. Pkt. 5c., oz. 10c., 1-4 lb. 30c., lb. $1.

Early Prize Head. The leaves are crisp and tender, and remain so throughout the season. Pkt. 5c., oz. 10c., 1-4 lb. 30c., lb. $1.

Grand Rapids. As a lettuce for greenhouse forcing, this variety stands at the head of the list, being of quick growth. The plant is upright and forms a loose head. Pkt. 5c., oz. 10c., 1-4 lb. 30c., lb. $1.00.

MELON. Musk.

Melons thrive best in a moderately rich, light soil.

Emerald Gem. This variety is of rich, delicious flavor and fine quality; very early and prolific; skin of a deep emerald green. The flesh is thick, salmon color. Pkt. 5c., oz. 10c., 1-4 lb. 15c., lb. 50c.

Nutmeg. Skin deep green; the flesh a greenish yellow, rich and sugary. Pkt. 5c., oz. 10c., 1-4 lb. 15c., lb 50c.

Early Hackensack. The popular variety of Musk Melon; very early; attains a good size; is of delicious flavor and wonderfully productive. Pkt. 5c., oz. 10c., 1-4 lb. 15c., lb. 50c.

MELON. Water.

Sweetheart. (See cut.) It is very large, a little longer than thick. Skin very bright; beautifully mottled green. Flesh bright red, firm and heavy, but crisp, melting and sweet. Pkt. 5c., oz. 10c., 1-4 lb. 15c., lb. 50c.

Mountain Sweet. Fruit oblong, dark green, rind thin, flesh red, solid and very sweet. Pkt, 5c., oz. 10c, 1-4 lb. 15c., lb. 40c,

Phinney's Early. Flesh red; good quality, early and productive. Pkt. 5c oz. 10c., 1-4 lb. 15c., lb. 40c.

ONION.

The onion thrives best in a rather deep, rich loomy soil, and unlike most vegetables succeeds well when cultivated on the same ground for successive years. The ground should be deeply trenched and manured the previous autumn, and laid up in ridges during the winter to soften. As early in the spring as the ground is in working order, commence operations by leveling the ground with a rake, tread it firmly; sow thinly in drills about a quarter of an inch deep and a foot apart; cover with fine soil, press down with the back of a spade or light roller. Keep the surface of the ground open and free from weeds by frequent hoeing, taking care not to stir the soil too deeply, or to collect it about the growing bulbs. If by mail in quantities of 1-2 lb. and upwards, add at the rate of 8c per lb.

Southport Yellow Globe. A handsome globular Onion, of mild flavor and a good keeper. One of the very best. Pkt. 5c., oz. 15c., 1-4 lb. 50c., lb. $1.50.

Southport White Globe. Handsome globular Onion of mild flavor.

One of the best. Pkt. 5c., oz. 20c., 1-4 lb 65c, lb. $2.50.

Griswold's Medium Early Red Globe. This is one of the best varieties of Onion grown for the market. It is nearly round in shape, having a bright red color, Medium Early, (ripening about two weeks before the Southport Red Globe,) very productive and a good keeper. Pkt. 5c , oz. 20c., 1-4 lb. 60c., lb. $2.25.

Yellow Globe Danvers. An excellent variety, mild. flavored and very productive; ripens early, and is

a good keeper. Pkt. 5c,oz. 15c 1-4 lb. 40c. lb. $1.30.

Wethersfield Large Red. Standard for eastern markets; of large size, deep red, and excellent keeper. Pkt. 5c, oz. 15c., 1-4 lb. 40c., lb. $1.30.

Larger lots at special rates.

PARSLEY.

Parsley succeeds best in a rich mellow soil. It should be sown early in spring, previously soaking the seed in tepid water.

Doubled Curled. A fine dwarf va-

25 Pkts. Vegetable Seeds for $1.00.

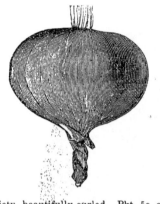

riety, beautifully curled. Pkt. 5c. oz. 10c.

PARSNIP.

Sow as early in spring as the weather will permit, in drills 15 inches apart, covering half an inch deep. When well up thin out to five or six inches apart in the rows. Unlike carrots they are improved by frost, and it is usual to take up in fall a certain quantity for winter use, leaving the rest in the ground until spring, to be dug as required.

Long Smooth or Hollow Crown Standard for general use. Pkt. 5c., oz. 10c., 1-4 lb. 15c. lb. 40c.

PEAS.

Ten cents pkt. Add at the rate of 15 cents per qt. if sent by mail.

McLean's Little Gem. A wrinkled variety, very early; quality good; 1 foot high. Pt. 15c; qt. 25c., pk. $1.10.

First and Best. Very desirable early variety, and ripens thoroughly; 2 feet high. Pt. 10c., qt. 20c., pk. $1.

Hosford's Market Garden. A wrinkled variety coming in between Little Gem and Advancer; 2 feet high. It is a prolific bearer, the pods of a medium size, and the peas are of a delicious sweet flavor. Pt. 10c., qt .20 cents, pk. $1.

McLean's Advancer. The best and second early pea for market or home use. Green, wrinkled and of delicious flavor; 2 feet high. Pt. 10c., qt. 20c., pk. $1.

Champion of England. One of the most popular sorts known; five feet high. Pt. 10c., qt. 20c , pk. $1.

Black-Eyed Marrowfat. A favorite in Boston markets; large pods; prolific; 5 feet high. Pt. 10c., qt. 15c, pk. 75c.

American Wonder. One of the earliest wrinkled peas in cultivation, fine quality and flavor; 10 inches in height. Pt. 15c, qt. 30c, pk $1.50.

Bliss Abundance Pea. Very productive; grows 15 to 18 inches; pods 3 to 3 1-2 inches long, well filled. excellent puality; a second early variety. The seeds should be sown thinner than usual. Pt. 10c, qt 20c, pk. $1.25.

Heroine. The Heroine is a medium early, green wrinkled Pea, grows about 2 1-2 feet high and is literally covered with its long, heavy, pointed pods. Rich flavor. Pt. 10c, qt. 20c, pk. $1.25.

Nott's Excelsior. An extra early dwarf wrinkled Pea, usually ready for table in 4o to 5o days from planting. only a few days later than the early round sorts. It grows about 14 inches high. It is wonderfully productive. Pt. 15c, qt. 25c, pk. $1.50.

Bliss' Ever Bearing A continuous bearing variety, which gives it especial value for late summer and autumn use; height 2 feet. Pt. 10c; qt. 20c, pk $1.25.

PEPPER.

Grown largely for pickles. Sow in Hot-bed early in April, and transplant to the open ground when the weather is favorable. They should be planted in warm mellow soil, in rows 18 inches apart. They may also be sowed in the open ground when danger of frost is past and the soil is warm and settled.

Sweet Mountain or Mammoth Rind thick, fleshy and tender; much used for pickling, stuffed like mangoes. Pkt. 5c, oz. 20c.

Large Bell or Bull Nose. An early kind; the standard variety, large. Pkt 5c, oz..20c.

Squash or Tomato Shape. Best for pickles; very mild,and thick flesh. Pkt. 5c, oz. 25c.

Long Red Cayenne. Very productive. Pkt. 5c, oz. 20c.

RADISH.

Radishes thrive best in light sandy loam. If by mail, add 8c per pound.

French Breakfast. Very mild and tender; best for forcing. Pkt. 5c. oz 10c, 1-4 lb. 15c, lb. 40c.

Long Scarlet Short Top. The standard variety. Pkt. 5c, oz. 10c, 1-4 lb. 15c, lb. 40c.

Early Scarlet Turnip. Round; about an inch in diameter, skin scarlet and flesh white. Pkt. 5c, oz. 10c 1-4 lb. 15c, lb. 40c.

White Tipped Early Scarlet Turnip. Bright scarlet, fading off to pure white at the base, and is tender, mild in flavor and early. Pkt. 5c, oz. 10c, 1-4 lb. 15c, lb. 40c.

SPINACH.

If by mail, add 8c per lb. for postage·

Thick Leaf. The standard variety; equally good for spring or fall sowing. Pkt. 5c, oz. 8c, 1-4 lb. 15c, lb. 30c

Long Standing. Except in the characteristic of standing along time before going to seed, this variety resembles the round leaf. Pkt. 5c, oz. 8c, 1-4 lb. 15c, lb. 30c.

SQUASH.

Like all vegetables of this class, it is useless to sow until the weather has become settled, and warm, light soils are best suited for their growth. Manure in ordinary manner by incorporating two or three shovelfuls of well-rotted manure with the soil for each hill. For the bush varieties, from three to four feet each way and for the running sorts from six to eight feet. If by mail add 8c per pound.

Mammoth Summer Crookneck In the Mammoth we have the delicious, buttery flavor of the original sort, but of double the size. Pkt. 5c., oz. 10c., 1-4 lb. 20c., lb. 45c.

Summer Crookneck. Early productive, good quality. Pkt. 5c., oz. 10c., 1-4 lb. 20c, lb. 40c.

Winter Crookneck. Flesh close grained, sweet, and fine flavored. Pkt. 5c., oz 10c., 1-4 lb. 20c, lb. 50c.

Boston Marrow. A much esteemed variety, coming in about ten days later than the Crookneck sorts; a good keeper. Pkt. 5c, oz. 10c , 1-4 lb. 20c., lb. 40c.

Essex Hybrid. It is one of the richest flavored, finest grained and sweetest squashes, and one of the best keepers. The flesh is thick, rich colored and solid. Pkt. 5c, oz. 10c, 1-4 lb. 20c, lb. 50c.

25 Pkts. Vegetable Seeds for $1.00.

Hubbard. Large sized, fine grained, dry and of the best flavor. Pkt. 5c, oz. 10c, 1-4 lb. 20c, lb. 50c.

Early Yellow Bush Scallop. An early, flat scallop shaped variety; color yellow; flesh pale yellow and well flavored. Pkt. 5c, oz. 10c, 1-4 lb. 20c, lb. 40c.

Marblehead. Much more productive and better quality than the famed Hubbard. Pkt. 5c, oz. 10c, 1-4 lb 15c, lb. 45c.

TOMATO.

The seed should be sown in a hot bed about the first of March, in drills five inches apart and half an inch deep. When the plants are about two inches high they should be set out four or five inches apart in another hot bed or removed into small pots, allowing a single plant to a pot. About the middle of May the plants may be set in the open ground

Livingstone's Favorite. It is one of the largest and most perfect shaped varieties in cultivation; ripens early. Pkt. 5c, oz. 20c.

Volunteer. Very early; productive and a fair size. Pkt. 5c, oz. 20c.

Peach. The fruit is uniform size, and resembles a peach in shape. Pkt. 5c, oz. 20c.

Table Queen. Perfectly smooth and round. It is solid and contains few seeds. The color is a rich crimson. Pkt. 5c, oz. 20c.

TURNIPS.

Turnips do best in a highly enriched, light, sandy or gravelly soil. If by mail, add eight cents per pound for postage.

Early Snowball. A round, pure white variety. For early sowing this is one of the best, being crisp, tender and sweet. Pkt. 5c, oz. 10c, 1-4 lb. 20c., lb. 60c.

Early Red Top Strap Leaf. One of the best for general use. Pkt. 5c, oz. 10c, 1-4 lb. 15c, lb. 42c.

Early Purple Top Milan. The earlist variety in cultivation. The color is bright reddish purple above ground and clear white underneath. Pkt. 5c, oz. 10c, 1-4 lb. 25c, lb. 60c.

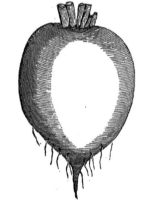

White Egg. A very excellent variety; flesh firm and of fine grain and of snowy whiteness. Pkt. 5c, oz. 10c, 1-4 lb. 15c, lb. 42c.

RUTA BAGA OR SWEEDISH.

The Ruta Baga or Sweedish Turnip is exclusively grown for a farm crop, and is excellent for the table early in the spring. Sow from the 20th of June to the middle of July.

Improved American. Yellow, solid and sweet, very productive. Pkt. 5c, oz. 10c, 1-4 lb. 15c. lb, 42c.

Breadstone. A very superior strain of white Ruta Baga, of medium size; smooth, quick growing, flesh fine grained, perfectly white, sweet and

25 Pkts. Vegetable Seeds for $1.00.

tender. Pkt. 5c, oz. 10c, 1-4 lb. 15c, lb. 42c.

SWEET AND POT HERBS.

Five cents per packet.

Sage. Broad leaved; oz. 15c.

SUMMER SAVORY. Oz. 15c.

CORIANDER. Oz. 10c.

THYME. Oz. 25c.

ANISE. Oz. 15c.

SWEET MAJORAM. Oz. 20c.

VEGETABLE PLANTS.

CABBAGE PLANTS.

For early setting started in spring.

	per 100.	per 1000
Early Jersey Wakefield. Ready April 15.	50c	$4.00
Henderson's Early Summer. Ready April 15.	50c.	$4.00

For fall and winter crops, ready July 1.

Autumn King.	30c.	$2.50
Premium Flat Dutch.	30c.	$2.50
Red. [For pickling.]	30c.	$2.50
Fottler's Drumhead.	30c.	$2.50

CAULIFLOWER.

	per doz.	per 100
Henderson's Early Snowball. Ready May 1.	20c.	$1.00

CELERY.

	per 100.	per 1000
Crawford's Half Dwarf. Ready June 15.	60c.	$5.00
White Plume. Ready June 15.	60c.	$5.00

PEPPER PLANTS.

	per doz.	per 100
Sweet Mountain. Ready May 15.	20c.	$1.25
Bull Nose. Ready May 15.	20c.	$1.25

TOMATO PLANTS.

	per doz.	per 100
Favorite. Pot plants. Ready May 15.	35c.	$2.50
Table Queen. Pot plants. Ready May 15.	35c.	$2.50
Volunteer, Pot plants. Ready May 15.	35c.	$2.50
☞Box plants at	20c.	1.25

25 Pkts. Vegetable Seeds for $1.00.

	Each	Dozen.
AGERATUM, blue and white,	8 cents.	$ .75
AMPELOPIS VEITCHII, south side ivy,	15 "	1.50
ASTERS, choice collection ready May 15th,	5 "	.25
BALSAMS, mixed, ready May 15th,	5 "	.25
BEGONIAS TUBEROUS, single flowers, mixed colors,	20 "	1.50
BEGONIAS, six varieties,	10 "	1.00
CALADIUM ESCULENTUM,	25 "	2.00
CALLA ETHIOPICA,	20 "	2.00
CANNA, French ever blooming,	15 "	1.00
CARNATIONS, in variety,	10 "	1.00
CHRYSANTHEMUMS in variety,	10 "	1.00
COLEUS, many colors and varities,	10 "	.75
CUPHEA, cigar plant,	10 "	.75
FEVERFEW,	10 "	.75
FUCHIAS, in variety, double and single,	10 "	1.00
GERANIUMS, double, all colors,	10 "	1.00
GERANIUMS, single all colors,	10 "	1.00
GERANIUMS, newer varieties,	15 "	1.50
GERANIUMS, double ivy leaved,	15 "	1.50
GERANIUMS, sented,	10 "	1.00
GLOXINIAS, mixed colors,	15 "	1.50
HELIOTROPES,	10 "	1.00
IVIES, German and English,	10 "	1.00
LEMON VERBENAS,	15 "	1.50
LOBELIAS,	8 "	.60
MAHERNIA ODORATA,	15 "	1.50
MANETTIA BICOLOR,	10 "	1.00
MOON FLOWER,	15 "	1.50
PANSIES, seeding from choice varieties,	5 "	25 and 50
PETUNIAS, double fringed in varieties,	15 "	1.50
PETUNIAS, single in variety,	10 "	1.00
PRIMULA, single, red and white,	15 "	1.50
RICHARDIA ALBA MACULATA,	15 "	1.50
ROSES, Tea and Monthly in variety,	15 "	1.50
STOCKS, mixed colors,	5 "	.25
SALVIA SPLENDENS,	10 "	.75
TUBEROSE, double pearl, dry roots,	5 "	50
VINCA, VARIEGATED MYRTLE,	10 "	1.00
VERBENAS, MAMMOTH, in twelve colors,	8 "	.60
ZINNIAS, mixed colors, ready May 15,	5 "	.25

☞A discount of 25 per cent. is allowed on any of the above named plants if bought at the green house.

Press of
WINDHAM COUNTY TRANSCRIPT,
Danielson, Conn.

Lightning Source UK Ltd.
Milton Keynes UK
UKHW020022181218
334174UK00013B/2143/P